The Hawaiian Monk Seal

Monte Costa

With Aloha
from
Patrick Ching
Kauai 2012

The Hawaiian Monk Seal

Patrick Ching

A Kolowalu Book

University of Hawaii Press / Honolulu

Printed in Singapore

08 09 10 11 12 13   7 6 5 4 3 2

Library of Congress Cataloging-in-Publication Data

Ching, Patrick, 1962–

The Hawaiian monk seal / Patrick Ching.

p. cm.

"A Kolowalu book."

Includes bibliographical references.

ISBN 978-0-8248-1622-3

1. Hawaiian monk seal. 2. Endangered species—Hawaii. I. Title.

QL737.P64C48 1995

599.74'8—dc20   94–12429

CIP

Designed by Paula Newcomb

Contents

A RARE DISCOVERY

I became aware of the existence of the Hawaiian monk seal in 1979, my junior year in high school. While breezing through a Time-Life book, I was stopped cold by a photograph of a seal lying on a tropical beach. It stared at me with big, dark eyes that seemed to see straight into my soul. As I read the accompanying text, I was astonished to learn that this was a Hawaiian seal—one that exists nowhere else on earth.

How could such a creature have eluded me all these years?

As I read on I learned of the endangered status of these seals and that they live almost exclusively on the remote atolls to the northwest of the main Hawaiian Islands.

I had seen those islands on maps before, but I never thought anything lived on them. It was soon apparent to me that there was a lot more to learn about Hawai'i and its wildlife than I was aware of. Even after closing the book I could clearly see the beckoning eyes of the seal.

At the time it seemed impossible that I would ever see a Hawaiian monk seal in the flesh, but I remember telling myself, "If ever I do I'll be one of the luckiest people on earth." The months that followed were filled with dreams about encountering a seal while swimming or surfing. Though I had these dreams often, I eventually filed them away amidst shelves of other dreams unlikely to happen. I had no way of knowing then what a profound influence this wonderful creature would have on my life.

I got my first real glimpse of the mysterious monk seal in 1982 when I was sent to French Frigate Shoals as a volunteer for the U.S. Fish & Wildlife Service. While standing at the boat dock on Tern Island, the largest island within the shoals, a dark figure swam toward me. I knew instantly what it was, and as it broke the surface it stared at me with those big, dark eyes that I had seen a hundred times in my dreams. This was a landmark event in my life, and I savored it thoroughly.

Since then I have had many opportunities to observe monk seals in the wild and have become familiar with many aspects of their multifaceted lives. The time I have spent living in remote field camps with seals as my neighbors has been a precious source of education and inspiration for me.

Now, as an employee of the U.S. Fish & Wildlife Service, I am sometimes called on to respond to reports of seal harassment. It makes me realize that in order for the seals to continue to coexist with people, it is essential that residents and visitors alike be made aware of their fragile situation. Nobody knows what the future holds for these delicate beings. Will they still be around for future generations to appreciate? Or will they suffer the irreversible plight of extinction that has befallen so many creatures in recent years?

I see in my mind the eyes of the seal ʻīlio-holo-kai, "the dog that runs in the sea." It is a vision that occupies my thoughts every day. I hope the world will be good to our beloved seals. May they always be able to live in peace.

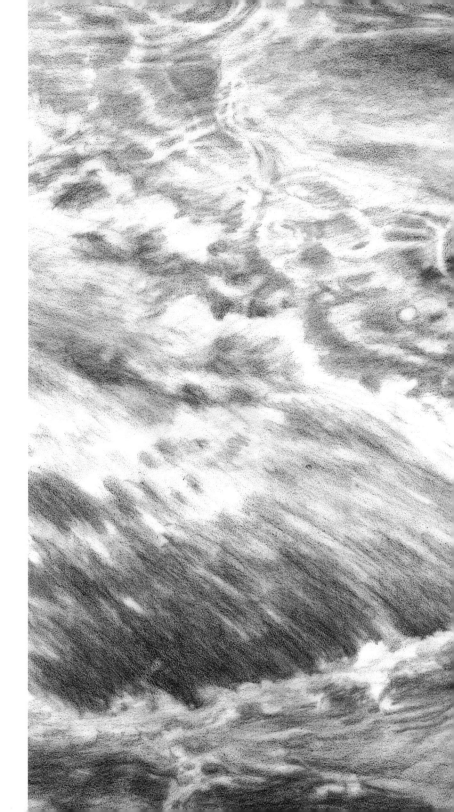

HISTORY

Virtually unchanged for millions of years, monk seals are the oldest and most primitive of all living pinnipeds (the order of fin-footed mammals that includes seals, walruses, and sea lions). Of the three known species of monk seals, only two survive today. Both are endangered.

The Hawaiian monk seal, *Monachus schauinslandi,* with an estimated population of fifteen hundred animals, has a much better chance of survival than its cousin, the Mediterranean monk seal, *Monachus monachus,* whose population is believed to be fewer than five hundred animals.

A third species, the Caribbean monk seal, *Monachus tropicalis,* was last sighted in 1952 and is now considered extinct. The Caribbean monk seal was almost identical in appearance to the Hawaiian seal, and if not for their geographic separation, the two may have been classified as the same species. The pressures of human disturbance and predation have had devastating effects on all three monk seal populations.

Scientists believe that the genus *Monachus* (monk seals) originated in the North Atlantic and ventured into the Caribbean, Mediterranean, and Pacific regions during a time in earth's history when a natural ocean passage existed between North and South America. About three million years ago the gap between the continents closed, leaving the monk seals in the Pacific permanently separated from those in the Caribbean.

Little is known about the Hawaiian monk seals' range prior to the colonization of the Hawaiian Islands by humans. It is possible that they inhabited the shores of all the Hawaiian Islands and perhaps even other areas of the Pacific. Surprisingly, there is virtually no mention of the seal in ancient Hawaiian chants or lore. Could such a unique creature have gone unnoticed? Probably not. A more likely explanation is that the seals disappeared from the main Hawaiian Islands as the Islands became populated by humans and therefore were seldom seen or remembered by the Islanders for hundreds of years. Though no evidence has been found that the Hawaiians of old traditionally killed or ate monk seals, that possibility should not be ruled out.

HAWAIIAN MONK SEAL
Monachus schauinslandi

CARIBBEAN MONK SEAL
Monachus tropicalis

MEDITERRANEAN MONK SEAL
Monachus monachus

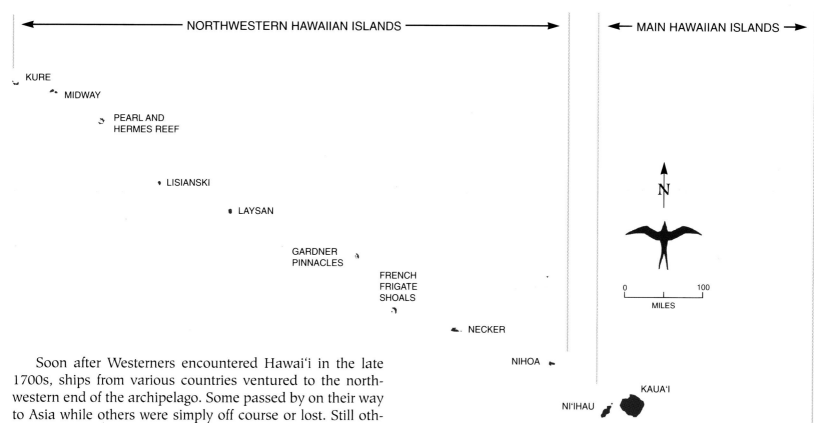

KURE

MIDWAY

PEARL AND
HERMES REEF

LISIANSKI

LAYSAN

GARDNER
PINNACLES

FRENCH
FRIGATE
SHOALS

NECKER

NIHOA

N

0   100
MILES

KAUA'I

NI'IHAU

O'AHU   MOLOKA'I

LĀNA'I   MAUI

KAHO'OLAWE

HAWAI'I

Soon after Westerners encountered Hawai'i in the late 1700s, ships from various countries ventured to the northwestern end of the archipelago. Some passed by on their way to Asia while others were simply off course or lost. Still others had specific purposes in mind. Throughout the nineteenth and early twentieth centuries, feather collectors, guano miners, and seal hunters had so severely exploited the natural resources of these remote islands that a number of plant and animal species had become extinct. Monk seals were killed for their meat, oil, and possibly their fur. By the early 1900s their numbers had become critically low.

Appalled by the pillaging and slaughter, President Theodore Roosevelt in 1909 designated the Northwestern Hawaiian Islands, with the exception of Midway atoll, as the Hawaiian Islands Reservation, giving the area protected status. In 1940 the islands from Nihoa to Pearl and Hermes Reef were renamed the Hawaiian Islands National Wildlife Refuge, managed by the U.S. Fish & Wildlife Service (USFWS).

In 1980 the National Marine Fisheries Service (NMFS) monk seal recovery program was initiated under the leadership of William Gilmartin to study Hawai'i's seals and aid in the recovery of the species. The Marine Mammal Commission, an independent U.S. agency, reviews the recovery efforts of the NMFS team.

INHABITING ANCIENT VOLCANOES

A scattering of reefs, atolls, and islets makes up the Northwestern Hawaiian Islands. These islands, which are sometimes referred to as the Leeward Islands, are all that remain of large volcanoes that towered high above the sea. Once abundant with mountains and streams, millions of years of erosion and sinking caused these islands to fall back into the sea, where coral reefs formed on top of them. As the coral broke down, large banks of sand were formed.

Most of the Leeward Islands are mere sand dunes rising only a few feet above sea level, some even disappearing during high tide. A few of the larger islands are covered with coastal vegetation. The only volcanic rock islands west of Ni'ihau are Nihoa and Necker Islands, and La Pérouse and Gardner pinnacles.

An atoll is an island or series of islets that lies upon a barrier reef, marking the spot where a large island once stood. Generally the farther west an island or atoll is located within the Hawaiian archipelago, the earlier in geological time it was formed. Kure, the oldest and westernmost atoll in the Hawaiian chain, is believed to be over thirty million years old. The island of Kaua'i is thought to be about five million years old, while Hawai'i (the Big Island) is less than one million years old and is still being formed.

Lisianski Island   Monte Costa

A sandspit that "disappears" during high tide. French Frigate Shoals.   Mitch Craig

WHAT'S IN A NAME?

Monk seals probably acquired their common name because of their bald appearance, solitary habits, and a fold of skin behind their heads that resembles a monk's hood.

The Hawaiian monk seal's scientific name, *Monachus schauinslandi,* is composed of the Greek word *monachus,* meaning "monk," and the last name of Dr. Hugo Hermann Schauinsland, who acquired the skull of the seal used to scientifically describe the species in 1905.

The oldest known Hawaiian name for seal, which appears in the Pukui and Elbert *Hawaiian Dictionary,* is *'īlio-holo-i-ka-uaua,* or "quadruped that runs in the rough [seas]."

On the island of Ni'ihau, a privately owned island where Hawaiian is the primary language, there are at least two names for the seal. According to Keith Robinson, whose family owns the island, "one is *sila,* derived from the word seal, and the other is *'īlio-holo-kai,* meaning 'the dog that runs in the sea.'"

MONKS ON THE MOVE

In the water, a monk seal moves with ease and grace—its rear flippers being the main source of propulsion. On land, however, its movement is anything but graceful, and traveling short distances seems to require a great deal of effort.

With fore flippers outstretched and barely touching the ground, a monk seal repeatedly heaves its cumbersome body forward in a motion referred to as "hauling." As it gains momentum, the seal may appear to bounce across the beach, leaving distinctive tracks behind. Scoop marks on either side of the tracks are made by the seal's fore flippers while lines in the center are formed by its dragging rear flippers.

During the heat of the day many monk seals move to the cool, wet sands near the water's edge to bask in the midday sun; at this time biologists conduct a beach count, or census. This census helps in determining the monk seal population. While most censuses are done on foot, some are conducted from a boat or by taking aerial photographs. Researchers estimate that the number of seals counted on shore represents one-third to one-half of the entire population.

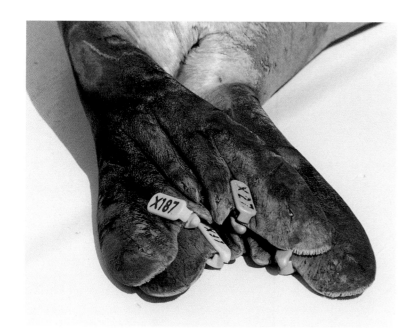

In 1966 the U.S. Fish & Wildlife Service began applying tags to the rear flippers of monk seals. The service continued to tag seals intermittently until the early 1970s. The NMFS began a tagging program in 1981, and since 1984 most of the newly weaned seals born in the Northwestern Hawaiian Islands have been fitted with plastic tags on their rear flippers. The tags are coded with letters and numbers, enabling researchers to identify individual seals so that they may better understand the monk seals' habits and needs and assess rehabilitation progress.

Most tags placed on seals are color coded; each island or atoll is represented by a different color. This enables researchers to determine which island a seal is originally from, thus making it easier to trace interisland movement patterns.

Some disadvantages of the plastic tags include the fading of colors over long periods of time and the abrasion of numbers or letters. And occasionally the tags get lost or are torn from the seals' flippers during skirmishes. Because of these shortcomings, alternative tagging procedures are constantly being investigated. One experimental tag, called a PIT (Passive Integrated Transponder) tag, is small enough to be injected under the seal's skin and can be read using an electromagnetic reading device.

If you see a monk seal with tags, contact your federal or state wildlife officials. Do not try to approach the seal to read its tags.

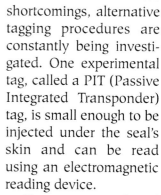

INTERACTION AND MATING

Generally speaking, monk seals are solitary animals. Although they do congregate and even "pal around" at times, they don't seem to keep the same company for very long. Even mated pairs soon drift apart—lengthy alliances are not the norm. Unlike many pinnipeds, male monk seals do not keep harems. Instead, they cruise the shallow waters along the shoreline in search of prospective mates.

When a "cruiser" approaches seals on shore, vocalizations are often exchanged. A guttural "bwoop bwoop bwoop" or belching "bwaaah!" are common utterances. The cruiser may then haul out onto the beach to investigate the situation. If there is an eligible female accompanied by another male, a skirmish may ensue between the males. When male seals fight to establish dominance, it is referred to as "jousting." These jousts are usually brief and rarely if ever result in serious injury or death. The match ends when the cruiser is either chased off or displaces the other male, thus claiming his dominance and a spot next to a prospective mate.

Adult monk seals of both sexes are similar in size, having total body lengths of approximately seven feet and weights averaging 450 pounds. Unless you get a good view of a monk seal's underside, you may find it difficult to determine its sex. Unlike females, however, males usually possess numerous jousting scars around the throat and neck.

Like some other mammals, male monk seals possess a baculum—a bone within the penis that is usually recessed beneath a slot located just below the navel. A faint line runs from the penal slot toward the base of the tail. This line is not present on female seals, who instead have four teats surrounding the navel.

Male

Female

Monk seals become sexually mature at about four to seven years of age. Compared to some other animals their courtship may seem rather blasé. Courting pairs are not known to exhibit elaborate rituals or fancy dances. Instead, they simply spend time together, lying around or swimming. The female is generally coy, not showing much interest in the male. On shore some muzzle nudging and vocalizing may occur, usually instigated by the male. In the water the pair may seem very playful, spinning in circles around each other or chasing one another in a game of tag, usually with the male in pursuit.

Mating takes place in the water. This event is rarely witnessed by humans and was first documented only as recently as 1978. It is common behavior for the male to bite ahold of the female's back during mating. This may result in slight injury to the female but under normal circumstances is not fatal.

Male approaching female

Monte Costa

11

MOTHERS AND PUPS

In the weeks prior to giving birth, a pregnant seal gorges herself with food. She becomes extremely obese and may weigh over six hundred pounds. The excess food is transformed into blubber and milk, which will sustain her and her pup throughout the nursing period.

Finding a suitable birth site is her next priority; ideally it will be somewhere close to shallow, protected waters. When the expectant mother chooses a birth site she may haul out and settle there for a few days before giving birth.

Most monk seal births occur during spring and summer; however, births have been documented during every month of the year. Most sexually mature females give birth every other year, although some individuals have been known to reproduce in consecutive years. A female monk seal well past the age of twenty may bear offspring. The actual birth process is brief, normally taking one to ten minutes from the time the pup's head appears till parturition is complete. Once the pup hits the ground, it tears out of its embryonic sack and takes its first breath of air. Mother and pup soon call to one another: mother with a deep bellowing "bwaaah" and pup with a high nasal "bwaaap!"

Glistening wet, the gangly pup is then nuzzled by its mother, who after a while rolls over to expose her four teats, which the pup eventually finds and suckles.

George H. Balazs

Jet black in color, the newborn pup weighs about thirty pounds. Its loose, velvety skin cloaks its body like an oversized coat.

The first few weeks of a pup's life are spent napping, nursing, and swimming in the shallows close to shore with its mother. During the nursing period, which normally lasts five to six weeks, the mother seal is constantly by her pup's side and does not go off to catch food for herself. By the end of the nursing period, both mother and pup will have gone through extreme physical changes.

WEEKS OF GIVE AND TAKE

Brenda Becker

USFWS

First week The pup's coat, still solid black, is loose and has many folds in it. Its head and limbs appear disproportionately large.

Second week As the pup's appetite increases, so does its size, and the folds in its coat begin to disappear.

Third week Mother seal begins to show weight loss as her pup grows rapidly. Patches of light gray fur may begin to appear on the pup's belly.

Fourth week Gray fur continues to replace the pup's black birth coat. Both mother and pup spend more time in the water.

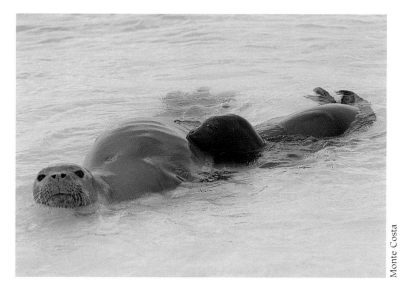

Fifth week Weeks of fasting have depleted the once obese mother to the point that the contours of her ribs are plainly visible through her skin. The pup, on the other hand, is now a roly-poly butterball with a tightly fitting gray coat.

Having cared for her pup for nearly forty days, the exhausted mother is ready to wean her pup. She has lost about half of her prebirth weight, and if she does not eat soon she will die. Her job complete, she quietly slips away, heading for open water to tend to her own nutritional needs. From this day on she will have nothing more to do with the pup, who must now learn to fend for itself.

15

The weanling's first attempts at catching fish are usually unsuccessful. Discouraged, it may then try for easier prey. Sea cucumbers seem to be a popular choice, as many newly weaned seals have muzzles strewn with the stringy white stuff that sea cucumbers squirt. As the young seal gets thinner it becomes quicker, more agile, and more adept at feeding itself; nonetheless, it continues to lose weight during its first year of life.

FAT TIMES

The newly weaned pup, or weanling, may weigh nearly five times what it did at birth. It is so fat from its mother's milk that it has difficulty moving about. Because of its lack of agility and its inexperience at catching food, it is at its most vulnerable period in life.

A weanling's excess body fat provides enough nourishment to last it for a while. Life seems carefree at first, and much of a weanling's time is spent sleeping or playing with other newly weaned seals. As time goes by and its stored body fat is used up, the young seal starts to think about a more serious pastime—finding food.

THE ANNUAL MOLT

Once a year a monk seal will come ashore to molt or shed its coat. The molting process takes about nine or ten days, during which time the seal spends almost all of its time on shore. The seal's fur looks dull brown or gray prior to molting. If algae has grown on it, it may even appear green or orange. After molting, the seal's new coat has a soft, silvery look.

A seal's annual molt is very different from the first molt it experienced as a pup. At that time, its coat gradually turned from black to gray as individual hairs fell off and were replaced. From the time it is a year old a seal molts its entire pelage: starting on its belly area, the old coat peels back and

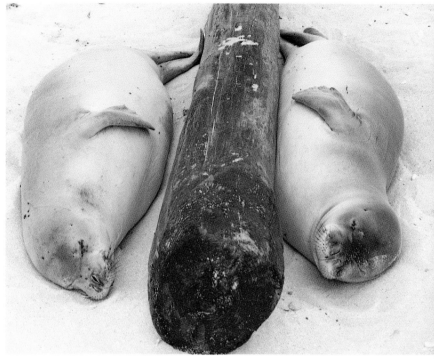

Old coat/new coat

falls away in patches. The last part of the body to molt is usually the middle of its back.

There is a general molting order among monk seals. The first to molt are the adult females, followed by subadult and juvenile females and juvenile males. Next in order are subadult males and females that have recently given birth. The last to molt are the yearlings of both sexes and adult males. Molting usually takes place between April and December.

NATURAL NEIGHBORS

Most of the world's monk seals live within the boundaries of the Hawaiian Islands National Wildlife Refuge. Here they share their domain with other animals, including sea turtles and a variety of native birds, some of which exist nowhere else on earth.

Interaction between species is a normal occurrence, and a seal will often bellow at a wandering bird that gets too close or snuggle up to a sleeping turtle.

Because human disturbance on the refuge is kept at a minimum, the animals can live in peace among their natural neighbors, each holding an important position in one of the last harmonious ecosystems in Hawai'i.

Young laysan albatross

George H. Balazs

A green sea turtle and seal napping together.

George H. Balazs

Male frigate bird in courtship display

Nesting red-footed booby

Masked boobies and sea turtles basking on the beach

George H. Balazs

LAZY ON LAND, SWIFT IN THE SEA

Basking in the midday sun is a favorite pastime of Hawaiian monk seals. Being nocturnal hunters, they spend most of their daylight hours lounging in bliss. Seals sneeze frequently, perhaps to clear parasitic nose mites that may be annoying them. Occasionally they release a deep, drawn out breath that often ends in a loud, wet snort.

Some seals even seem to talk in their sleep. Though their mouths may be closed, a rhythmic thumping of baritone notes resounds from within. These noises sound more like a kid playing a tuba than a seal. One can only wonder what kind of dreams a seal could have to induce such a sound.

Because they appear so lethargic, many people who see monk seals lying on the shore think they are sick or dead. Actually, they are just getting their much-needed rest and should not be approached or disturbed.

While their mobility is limited on land, monk seals are remarkably nimble in the water. Their sleek bodies enable them to dart and swivel about at high speeds or cruise along gracefully, wagging their large rear flippers from side to side.

Being able to move so freely makes them confident in their liquid element. Their curious nature will sometimes bring them within arms' reach of a swimmer. Though seals are not usually aggressive toward humans, don't let those big eyes and cute faces fool you; even a playful seal can inflict a nasty bite.

SEALS' MEALS

Being opportunistic feeders, monk seals do most of their foraging at night, when many sea creatures emerge from their daytime hiding places. A monk seal's meals may include such delicacies as lobster, eel, octopus, and a wide variety of reef fish—sometimes even small sharks!

By placing depth-recording devices on a number of seals, scientists obtain information such as how many dives the seals make and how deep they dive. This information is important in determining what steps should be taken to preserve the seals' feeding grounds. The deepest dive recorded was over eight hundred feet. That's a long way to go for a seafood dinner!

Bruce Eilerts

CROWDING ON THE SHOALS

French Frigate Shoals, situated over four hundred miles west of Kaua'i, is a crescent-shaped atoll named after two French frigate ships that nearly ran aground there in 1786. It is the closest true atoll to the main Hawaiian Islands and home to about one-third of all monk seals in Hawai'i.

In the mid-1900s the shoals were used by commercial fishing companies and later as a site for navy and coast guard operations. The presence of humans had obvious effects on the monk seal, whose population diminished and remained low until the military's departure in 1979. Since then the atoll has been turned over to the U.S. Fish & Wildlife Service, and the monk seal population has increased steadily, reaching a peak in 1986, when over nine hundred seals were thought to reside there.

A malnourished yearling

In recent years an alarming phenomenon has occurred at French Frigate Shoals. Many of the seals there are suffering from severe malnutrition, some to the point where they can no longer feed themselves and so eventually die. One explanation for this occurrence may be that the seals at the shoals have reached their population capacity and the limited food supply can therefore no longer sustain their numbers. If this is the case, it has not been known to happen on any of the other atolls. Since 1987 pup production and the total seal population at French Frigate Shoals have been significantly reduced. Only time will tell whether or not this downswing is just part of a natural fluctuation. Meanwhile, researchers are keeping a watchful eye on the situation.

Susan Scott

24

A pup gets displaced

Brenda Becker

Three pups nurse from one mother

Mitch Craig

Another problem that occurs frequently in densely populated areas is "pup switching." This event is most common on beaches shared by a number of mother-pup pairs.

A hungry pup may attempt to nurse from a seal other than its own mother. The lactating female, apparently confused over the identity of the pup, may nurse it as her own. Should the female reject her original pup, it must then find another lactating female, usually the one from which the first pup just came.

A mother seal produces only enough milk to last the normal six-week nursing period. Therefore, if the switched pups are of different ages, then one of the pups will be weaned prematurely while the other may continue to nurse well past the normal six-week period. The prematurely weaned pup has a poor chance of survival and, unless it is helped, will likely die.

An ongoing project of the NMFS is to rescue prematurely weaned and emaciated seals, rehabilitate them in captivity, and reintroduce them to areas within the Hawaiian Islands chain where seal numbers are low.

HEADING DOWN THE CHAIN

Ni'ihau is the only privately owned island in Hawai'i. Access to Ni'ihau is prohibited without permission from the Robinson family, who holds the deed to the island. Most of Ni'ihau's residents are of Hawaiian ancestry. The island is also home to some native plants and animals, including monk seals. Government biologists do not conduct field studies on Ni'ihau because of its private ownership; therefore, there is little data on the monk seals there.

According to Keith Robinson, monk seals were virtually nonexistent around Ni'ihau prior to 1970. But on 5 December of that year, while assisting in a search for a missing boat named the *Bonito*, a group of Robinson's men came upon a seal resting on the reef at Lehua Rock just off Ni'ihau. "The men were terrified of it," said Robinson. "None of them had ever seen one before." After that sighting, the number of monk seals around Ni'ihau gradually increased, reaching a peak in 1991, at which time, Robinson estimates, there were about fifty fat, healthy seals using the island. Since then, there's been a noticeable decline in the seal population, perhaps due to large predaceous sharks that have been sighted around the island.

Previously off-limits to anyone except residents, their families, and invited guests, Ni'ihau is now open to the public via the Robinsons' private helicopter tours. "The chopper was purchased primarily in case of medical emergencies," Robinson said. "But helicopters are very expensive so we started the tours to help defray the cost. We don't fly near the populated section of the island but we do land at a spot where seals are often seen."

Monk seals are basically "homebodies." Most of them never stray far from the islands of their birth. A few, however, do journey great distances between islands, and some indi-

The island of Ni'ihau

Monte Costa

26

viduals have even been sighted as far away as the Johnston, Palmyra, Wake, and Bikini Islands—up to two thousand miles from Hawai'i.

With the exception of these few individuals, the known historic range of the Hawaiian monk seal has been almost entirely restricted to the Northwestern Hawaiian Islands, with sightings around the main islands extremely rare.

The first documented birth of a monk seal on one of the major Hawaiian Islands was in 1961 at Polihale Beach on Kaua'i. Throughout the 1980s it was still very rare to see a seal on or around the populated Hawaiian Islands, so it came as quite a surprise when a seal was born on Kaua'i's south shore in 1988. Since that time monk seal sightings have become increasingly regular around the main Islands, espe-

cially on Kaua'i. The reasons for this are not totally understood. Perhaps with seal populations increasing at French Frigate Shoals and Ni'ihau it should be expected that some of those seals would venture farther down the chain.

The summer of 1991 was another highlight in monk seal history, when two seals were born on the main Islands—one each on the north shores of O'ahu and Kaua'i. Under the watchful eyes of volunteers who guarded the pups from a distance, both pups were successfully weaned.

By the mid-1990s, the island of Kaua'i was home to about a half-dozen resident seals. What was once a freak occurrence is now becoming almost common as more seals are hauling out onto beaches that for so many years have been the domain of humans.

A monk seal cruises Kāne'ohe Bay

Lenny Nichols, L. A. Film

SPECTACLE ON THE BEACH

When a monk seal appears on a populated beach it usually attracts a lot of attention. Some curious observers may approach the seal in order to take its picture or prod it simply to see it move. Dogs also harass resting seals, who usually retreat into the water when disturbed. Whenever a seal is chased into the water it is not only being deprived of its needed rest but is unnecessarily being forced into the sea, where it is vulnerable to shark attacks.

In 1976 Hawaiian monk seals were designated "depleted" under the Marine Mammals Act of 1972 and "endangered" under the Endangered Species Act of 1973. These acts made it a federal crime to kill, harm, or harass the seals.

State and federal laws also require people and their pets to maintain a distance of one hundred feet or more from a seal on shore. If you see a monk seal being bothered, ask the people involved to leave it alone and contact your state or federal wildlife officials or the police.

Whether or not the seals continue to haul out on the shores of the main Hawaiians Islands will depend largely on the actions and attitudes of Hawai'i's people.

Brian Chmielecki

A monk seal visits a Maui resort

Seals basking at Poʻipū Beach, Kauaʻi

David S. Boynton

Shark attack victim

DISEASE, DANGER, AND DEATH

In the wild, monk seals may live to be thirty years old. Causes of death (human factor aside) include shark attack, fish poisoning, and ailments associated with old age.

Necropsies performed on old seals reveal that they are often afflicted with stomach and intestinal parasites and dental disorders. Outbreaks of fish poisoning may be responsible for mass die-offs like the one that occurred on Laysan Island in 1978, in which over fifty seals perished. Some of the dead seals were found to have high levels of ciguatera, a toxin believed to originate in a certain blue-green algae that is passed along the aquatic food chain and accumulates in reef fish.

Sharks, the Hawaiian monk seals' only natural predator, are probably responsible for more seal deaths than all other causes combined. Tiger sharks are especially notorious for attacking seals. Many monk seals bear large scars from encounters with sharks; some even have missing flippers. These scars or missing limbs are often the best way for field biologists to identify individual seals.

A tiger shark attacks

Gray reef sharks circling at Laysan Island

THE ENEMY WITHIN

In the normal scheme of things, nature provides a harmonious balance. That is to say, for every male born there should be an almost equal number of females. For reasons unknown, the sex ratio of Hawaiian monk seals has become grossly uneven on some islands, with males significantly outnumbering females. In some locations, the number of males runs especially high, and so do aggressive sexual instincts. These are the areas where a gruesome event called "mobbing" takes place.

A mobbing incident may start out as a normal mating event between a pair of seals in the water. The action soon catches the attention of other males on the beach, and before long the female is surrounded by a mob of sex-crazed males. During the melee the frenzied males bite and tear into the female's back as they mount her in succession. The mobbing may involve over twenty-five males and last for hours, during which time the female may sustain massive, gaping wounds. Ravaged, she will likely die from her injuries or fall prey to sharks attracted by the smell of her blood.

Adult females are not the only victims of mobbings. Seals of both sexes and all ages have been killed by such attacks.

Easing the mobbing problem is a top priority of the NMFS monk seal recovery program, which is currently investigating the phenomenon and experimenting with ways to curb it. Meanwhile, more females fall victim to mobbing, thus compounding the problems of an already struggling species.

Mobbing victim

A mobbing in progress

NMFS

THE HUMAN FACTOR

For centuries, human impact has been a major factor in the decline of all monk seal populations. Though laws have been passed and refuges established, present-day seals continue to die at the hands of humans or from man-made devices.

Fish nets trap and kill a number of seals each year. Often commercial fishing ships at sea will discard broken nets by throwing them overboard. The nets may drift for years in the ocean, trapping and killing marine animals until they finally wash ashore or come to rest on the ocean floor.

Nets that drift ashore are a hazard because seals like to snuggle up to them. A curious seal will often inspect a net that has washed ashore by shoving its nose into the mass. If it gets caught in the net, it will likely strangle itself or die from heatstroke or starvation. Nets in the water also pose a threat because seals that try to eat fish caught in the nets may become snared themselves and drown.

Occasionally a seal will get caught on a fishing line while trying to eat the bait. Most recreational fishing rigs are not equipped to handle a seal, and the animal breaks free with the hook lodged firmly in its mouth. Longline fishing is especially deadly, as fishing vessels set adrift miles of baited fishing lines that indiscriminately kill monk seals and other marine animals along with the intended catch of fish.

Seals resting against drift net   NMFS

Fish hook lodged in seal's mouth   USFWS

Seal entangled in net   NMFS

In 1991 the Western Pacific Regional Fishery Management Council established a "protected species zone" prohibiting longline fishing within fifty nautical miles of the Northwestern Hawaiian Islands, including the corridors between the islands.

33

GIVING SEALS A HEAD START

Since its establishment in 1980, the NMFS monk seal recovery program has been looking into ways to increase the population of Hawai'i's endangered seal. An important phase of this project was the Head Start program, which began on the westernmost atoll of Kure in 1981. The monk seal population on Kure declined sharply during the late 1950s and early 1960s following the construction and occupation of a coast guard LORAN (LOng RAnge Navigation system) radar station. Even with new regulations to minimize human disturbance, the monk seal population remained low. In years prior to Head Start, nearly all of the pups born on Kure disappeared within their first year. The reasons for this are not known, although biologists suspect that sharks and aggressive adult seals were largely responsible.

Delivering live fish to hungry seals

Monte Costa

The goal of Head Start was to increase the survival rate of female pups born on Kure by keeping them in an enclosed area of the lagoon throughout their first summer. Within the confines of the enclosure the weaned pups learned to catch live food while they were kept safe from predaceous sharks and aggressive adult seals. By the time they were released, the young seals were strong and agile and more able to defend themselves against attack.

In 1987 the first of the Head Start seals gave birth on Kure. Since then many more have successfully pupped, and the monk seal population within the atoll has increased significantly and is expected to continue its recovery. The Head Start program was discontinued—in part because it successfully accomplished its goals—in 1991. In 1993 the coast guard's LORAN station was also shut down.

A weanling's first day out

David S. Boynton

from disturbance, but some local teachers even brought their classes to learn about the seals as they watched them from a distance. Even the most wandering minds were totally captivated as the children listened to the NMFS representative whisper facts about the seals.

Events like those just discussed are precious indeed as many people are experiencing the joy of watching monk seals in the wild without causing them stress. Something magical happens when people actually get to see an endangered animal in real life. It instills within them a sense of protective enthusiasm, thus strengthening conservation efforts.

Not everyone is fortunate enough to see a monk seal in the wild; however, anyone can get an excellent view of these incredible creatures at the Waikiki Aquarium or Sea Life Park. If you go to see the seals you will want to bring a camera. And be careful—one look into those big, dark eyes and you, too, could become an incurable monk seal "groupie."

FOR THE SAKE OF A SEAL

The implementation of state and federal laws protecting marine mammals was a major step toward the recovery of the Hawaiian monk seal population. As we well know, laws alone cannot protect a species. People must understand the laws and believe in their purpose in order for them to be effective.

As seals visit the main Hawaiian Islands more frequently, public awareness is increasing, and many people are taking the initiative to protect the seals from disturbance by simply asking spectators to observe them from a distance. Certain beachfront hotels are also pitching in to preserve the seals' solitude by roping off and placing educational signs around areas where seals haul up.

When a seal was born on a beach on O'ahu's north shore in 1991, the NMFS recruited the help of over fifty volunteers who guarded the mother and pup from a distance twenty-four hours a day throughout the entire nursing period.

Meanwhile, on Kaua'i's north shore, a similar scene took place with a pup that was born just six weeks after the one on O'ahu. Not only did the community rally to protect the seals

Monk seal exhibit at Sea Life Park, O'ahu   Facing page: Monte Costa

Monte Costa

Acknowledgments

The Hawaiian Monk Seal is a book I have envisioned for a long time. Many people contributed to making the vision become a reality. I cannot mention them all by name, but for all of those who helped, please know that your efforts have been sincerely appreciated.

I am especially grateful to William Gilmartin and the members of the National Marine Fisheries Service Monk Seal Research staff, not only for the help they have given me but for their dedication to preserving the species.

I also thank the staff of the U.S. Fish & Wildlife Service, Lorin Gill and the Moanalua Gardens Foundation, Donald Heacock of the state of Hawaii Department of Land and Natural Resource's Division of Aquatic Resources on Kaua'i, and Keith Robinson of the Robinson family of Ni'ihau.

To my friends and family who have helped me in so many ways, I am extremely grateful; especially to my sister Colette, who spent countless hours at the computer, which I have yet to figure out.

Finally, I thank everyone who cares about Hawai'i's unique and precious wildlife, for you are the ones who have made, and will continue to make, a difference.

Further Reading

Balazs, George H. *Hawaii's Seabirds, Turtles & Seals.* Honolulu: World Wide Distributors Ltd., 1976.

Kramer, Raymond J. *Hawaiian Land Mammals.* Rutland, VT, and Tokyo: Charles E. Tuttle Company, Inc., 1971.

Tomich, Quentin P. *Mammals in Hawaii.* Honolulu: Bishop Museum Press, 1986.

Van Riper, Sandra G. and Charles III. *A Field Guide to the Mammals in Hawaii.* Honolulu: The Oriental Publishing Company, 1982.

Hawaiian Wildlife Coloring Books by Patrick Ching
Native Animals of Hawaii. Honolulu: Bess Press, 1988.
Exotic Animals in Hawaii. Honolulu: Bess Press, 1988.
Beautiful Birds of Hawaii. Honolulu: Bess Press, 1992.

About the Author

Patrick Ching is an accomplished artist from Hawai'i whose artwork depicting native Hawaiian wildlife has been displayed internationally. Much of his energy is dedicated toward educating people about Hawai'i's unique and fragile ecosystem.

Ching works part time on Kaua'i and on the remote Northwestern Hawaiian Islands for the U.S. Fish & Wildlife Service, and he is a volunteer with the National Marine Fisheries Service monk seal recovery program.

He studied at Leeward Community College, the Otis/Parsons Art Institute in Los Angeles, and the University of Hawaii. Ching writes and illustrates "Naturally Hawaiian," a monthly column for the Office of Hawaiian Affairs newspaper, and he is the author/artist of three Hawaiian animal coloring books.

Steve Gregg

David S. Boynton